Y0-CCP-204

The first step of the test interpretation is to analyze the order of preference you selected for the shapes, Position 1 to 5. As you numbered the shapes according to your preference, you created a current map of your own inner landscape, giving an overview of your aspirations, resources, needs, and fears. The descriptions that follow on the back of the cards explain the meaning of each position in relation to the shape you placed in each position.

Position 1 | WHERE YOU THINK YOU ARE

The shape placed here, in this most preferred position, signals the process that now has your attention; it describes the part of yourself of which you are most aware and with which you are most comfortable at this time. The shape in Position 1 indicates your idea of the future or, perhaps, your current source of inspiration.

Position 2 | YOUR STRENGTHS

The shape you have chosen as your second preference exhibits an inherent strength predominant in you at this time, whether you know it or not. You demonstrate this strength to other people without effort. The shape in this position indicates areas of your nature that are currently fluid, strong, and resourceful. This shape reveals the innate talents you are using to assist the growth occurring in Position 3. Many people, who have taken this test, report that recent positive feedback and compliments they have received from others correspond to the qualities of the shape found in Position 2.

Position 3 | WHERE YOU ARE

Though this shape is third in your order of preference, it is the most significant: the shape you put in this position shows your true current growth process. This shape stands for the work that is really going on, right now, at the core of your being. Very often this process is unconscious or overlooked, yet you must be aware of it in order to fully manifest the potential it represents. The shape in this position can be a source of unlimited creativity and healing when you support the process it signifies. Now that you have discovered this shape in this meaningful position, you will be able to consciously acknowledge its visual presence and significance in your life.

Position 4 | YOUR MOTIVATION

Position 4 points to past challenges, tests, and circumstances that have motivated your current process of change. The fourth position of preference and the shape within it discloses the motivation that triggered your move into the core work to be done that is symbolized by the shape in Position 3. This shape furnishes clarifying information about the underlying incentive that has provoked you to do things differently now.

Position 5 | OLD, UNFINISHED BUSINESS

This shape, your least preferred, identifies a process you have outgrown or one that you dislike, still resist, or are judging. It indicates old, perhaps unfinished business. This fifth position is associated with unresolved issues you now wish to put aside. The shape placed here carries a process that you will reclaim and integrate at a later date. When you see the shape in the world around you, you may feel disinterested, or even irritated. You seldom want to be reminded of the process it represents.

THE TRIANGLE

Goals Dreams Visions

The Triangle is associated with pyramids, arrowheads, and sacred mountains. It carries the theme of self-discovery and revelation. This shape stands for goals, visions, and dreams.

People experiencing the triangular process are intensely focused on identifying and pursuing a goal; attaining it is extremely important to them. They have the innate gift of vision and their greatest need is to follow their dreams. Their worst fear is that there will be no dreams to pursue. They will persevere despite substantial obstacles and delays for as long as their goals have meaning for them. They need, however, to avoid becoming so absorbed in their plans for the future that they accomplish nothing in the present. That is a pitfall of the triangular process if it is taken to excess.

The triangle is the universal shape associated with the attainment of desired goals, and with the ability to envision new possibilities. Success in revisioning can lead to a burst of energy for new pursuits.

TEST INTERPRETATION

position 1

WHERE YOU
THINK YOU ARE

The process of envisioning seems most significant for you now.
You desire to manifest certain goals and dreams within reachable
time-frames.

position 2

YOUR
STRENGTHS

It indicates that you carry the gift of vision naturally, though
you may be unaware of that. Your behavior indicates to
others that you are a visionary, that you can create goals and
attain them.

position 3

WHERE YOU
ARE

The triangle means that the process of envisioning is central
to your current development. It is essential for you to honor
the goals and dreams that are important to you.

position 4

YOUR
MOTIVATION

This denotes that your own process of following dreams in the
past motivated you to make meaningful changes in your life.
Past visions and goals prepared and inspired you to move in the
direction of your core work in the present, designated by the
shape you have placed in position 3.

position 5

OLD,
UNFINISHED
BUSINESS

You may be resisting the process of honoring your dreams and
establishing goals. The need to manifest your goals or to
envision new possibilities is not a desired process for you now.

*Refer to meaning of positions on inside cover.

The Preferential Shapes Test © by Angeles Arrien 1992

THE PREFERENTIAL SHAPES TEST
SELECTION CARD

In order to find out your present and future processes of change and growth, draw the shapes SQUARE, TRIANGLE, CIRCLE, SPIRAL and CROSS on the placement lines #1 - #5. Number 1 will be your most preferred shape and Number 5 will be your least preferred shape.

Name: _____

1	2	3	4	5
___	___	___	___	___

Draw shapes in order of your preference on the lines above.

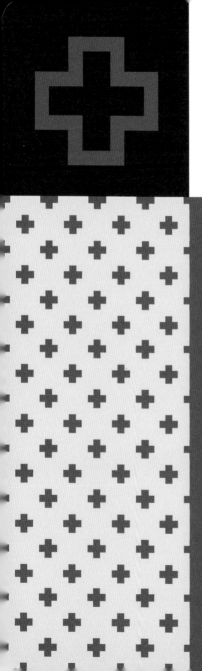

THE CROSS

Relationship

The equidistant cross, the plus sign, universally symbolizes the process of relationship and integration. This is a coupling, synthesizing, integrating and balancing process. This process carries the need for connection to a creative project, to a group, to another person, or to oneself. It is the symbol that demonstrates integration and balanced connection.

People who favor the cross will place emphasis on the quality, not the quantity, of time shared with others. Experiencing balance will be an essential goal for them. These individuals will often ask for a specific meeting time; they love collaborative work; and they equate quality of time spent in the company of close friends and colleagues with love and trust.

In most societies the cross is viewed as a religious symbol. In many others, it is not. Most societies see the symbol of the cross as two parts merging to create a greater whole.

TEST INTERPRETATION

position 1

WHERE YOU
THINK YOU ARE

It means that the process of relationship is what you believe to be most important in your life.

position 2

YOUR
STRENGTHS

It indicates that the shared journey is currently an effortless process for you, though you may not know this. Your behavior makes it obvious to others that your strength is in people skills, that you develop relationships easily, and that achieving balance is natural to you.

position 3

WHERE YOU
ARE

The cross shows that the relationship process is occurring deep within your nature. When you participate fully in this process, your originality and regenerative powers will be fully available to you.

position 4

YOUR
MOTIVATION

This makes clear that a past shared journey inspired you to become more attentive to partnership and teamwork endeavors. The past challenge that stimulated you to begin your core work in the present as designated by the shape in position 3.

position 5

OLD,
UNFINISHED
BUSINESS

This denotes you may want to ignore or dismiss the importance of the process of relationship in your life.

*Refer to meaning of positions on inside cover.

The Preferential Shapes Test © by Angeles Arrien 1992

THE SPIRAL

Growth and Change

The spiral symbolizes the process of growth and evolution. It is a process of coming to the same point again and again, but at a different level, so that everything is seen in a new light. The result is a new perspective on issues, people, and places.

Those involved in the spiral process have a strong need for variety, novelty, and change. They dread routine and they are capable of doing multiple tasks well. Creative and ingenious, they are adept at initiating and following up on projects, although they may have some difficulty completing them. The challenge of this process is to grow and develop at different levels of awareness. During times of change, creativity is required to handle life's situation and challenges with integrity.

position 1

WHERE YOU
THINK YOU ARE

It shows that the process of growth is the one you believe to be the most important for you at this time. You want to develop flexibility, to handle situations differently from the way you have in the past, and to implement tangible changes in your life.

position 2

YOUR
STRENGTHS

It denotes that it is easy for you to handle change, whether you know this or not. Your actions let others see that your strengths are flexibility and the ability to do many things at once.

position 3

WHERE YOU
ARE

It symbolizes that you are profoundly engaged in the process of change. It is essential to honor the changes occurring within your nature. Change and variety are necessary in your life. When you are able to trust this process, great energy will be released into all areas of your life.

position 4

YOUR
MOTIVATION

This lets you know that you were challenged in the past to make significant changes in your life. Meeting those challenges readied you for your current breakthrough work as shown by the shape in Position 3.

position 5

OLD,
UNFINISHED
BUSINESS

This means you are unlikely to show interest in the process of growth and change.

Working with the information you have gathered about your level of preference for the spiral will bring into focus that area of your inner map which depicts growth.

*Refer to meaning of positions on inside cover.

The Preferential Shapes Test © by Angeles Arrien 1992

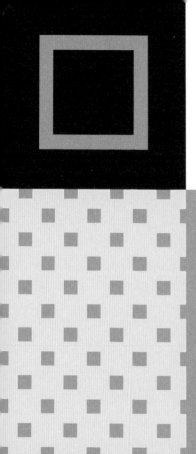

THE SQUARE

Stability

The square symbolizes stability, solidity, and security. The act of drawing a square mirrors perfectly the process of constructing a foundation.

Those attracted to the square are ready to build, to implement a plan, and to manifest ideas. These people have a strong need for consistency, accountability, and completion. They value integrity and authenticity, as well as responsibility and accountability. Congruity is especially important to them.

Whenever the square appears in art, and whenever examples of foundation metaphors are expressed in myths, the process of stability is being reinforced. The desire for security and congruity indicates that the person is experiencing the square process. When solid foundations exist, creativity, responsibility, and authenticity are usually present.

TEST INTERPRETATION

position 1

WHERE YOU
THINK YOU ARE

Stability and authenticity have your attention and are sources of inspiration to you. You value the alignment of words and actions.

position 2

YOUR
STRENGTHS

It indicates that your inherent strengths are responsibility, authenticity, and the ability to be fully committed when you give your word.

position 3

WHERE YOU
ARE

The square means that the process of stability is occurring at the core of your nature. It is vitally important for you to stabilize and implement your creative endeavors.

position 4

YOUR
MOTIVATION

This announces that past issues of responsibility and accountability led you to make substantial changes in your life. Past situations requiring consistency and stability prepared and motivated you to move in the direction of your present core work as shown by the shape in position 3.

position 5

OLD,
UNFINISHED
BUSINESS

This denotes you may be denying the process of stability and responsibility. The need to be consistent and congruent is not a primary focus for you, nor are you interested in exploring it now. The importance of stability and responsibility will become more clear to you as a result of exploring the meaning of your preference for the square.

*Refer to meaning of positions on inside cover.

The Preferential Shapes Test © by Angeles Arrien 1992

THE CIRCLE

Wholeness

In every culture the circle symbolizes wholeness and the experience of unity. When people are engaged in the search for wholeness they aspire to independence and individuation. What they need most is space, room in which to find themselves and develop their own identity. What they fear most is entrapment, being caught in a situation that will restrict or restrain them.

Those who are undergoing the process of individuation will feel loved and trusted when allowed plenty of space. If the space they need is not offered to them, they will simply take it. When the process of individuation is resisted or not allowed to come to resolution, it may become intensely self-absorbing, sometimes even narcissistic.

TEST INTERPRETATION

position 1

WHERE YOU
THINK YOU ARE

It indicates your desire to be independent and self-sufficient.

position 2

YOUR
STRENGTHS

It means that the heroic journey currently is effortless for you, whether or not you are aware of that. Your heroic behavior points out to others that your strengths are self-reliance and resourcefulness.

position 3

WHERE YOU
ARE

The circle shows that the process of individuation is occurring at the core of your nature. When fully engaged, this process of achieving and experiencing independence will allow your natural creative and restorative abilities to flow into all areas of your life.

position 4

YOUR
MOTIVATION

This denotes that a past heroic journey motivated you to become responsible and self-reliant. The process of individuation was the past challenge that caused you to move to your present core work (defined by the shape you have placed in Position 3).

position 5

OLD,
UNFINISHED
BUSINESS

You may be resisting or denying the process of individuation. The heroic journey currently does not have your attention and you have no interest in exploring it at this time.

*Refer to meaning of positions on inside cover.

The Preferential Shapes Test © by Angeles Arrien 1992

THE INSTRUCTIONS

In order to discover your present and future processes of change and growth, please take the following Preferential Shapes Test before you read the information on the individual cards.

INSTRUCTIONS FOR TAKING THE PREFERENTIAL SHAPES TEST

The five universal shapes are:
circle, square, triangle, cross, spiral.

Step 1
Draw the shapes listed above on a sheet of paper, or use the enclosed Preferential Shapes Test Selection Card.

Step 2
Number the shapes 1 through 5 in the order of your preference. Number 1 will be your most preferred shape and number 5 will be your least preferred shape. Please make your preferential choices before you read further.

Step 3
To interpret your test results, it is best to follow this order:

- Lay out the cards by shape in the numerical order of your preference.

- Read the symbol side first.

- Then turn the card over, keeping it in the same order, and read the information in the corresponding position for the insight into your current inner and outer experiences.

- To complete the process, read the full description of the Meaning of the Position under this panel. Read this information (under the panel) only after the above is completed!

assisting transformation in current life situations. Results from the test also revealed that shapes preferences are a good barometer of inner processes. The five shapes, I concluded, are indeed external symbols of internal psychic states

The preference for particular shapes is an announcement of the values and processes active at any time for an individual, a group, or a whole society. As one becomes sensitive to the shapes, one will see them in many forms, such as in doodles, business cards, corporate logos, and art collections. Modern architect Mies van der Rohe tells us, "Architecture is the will of the age conceived in spatial terms.".

The meaning ascribed to each of the five shapes symbolizes and demonstrates an individual's or a culture's world view: the qualities, characteristics, beliefs structures, actions and forms of expression used by one person or shared by the member of a society. The Preferential Shapes Test allows a person to discover one's own current world view. The information on the cards can also lead to a greater understanding of the world view of other individuals, of one's own culture, and of other cultures.

The sequence in which someone places the shapes when taking the test is most important in showing which of the five universal processes of change and growth is being experienced most intensely by that person at that time.

The value and meaning of the five shapes and their undeniable presence in our lives was recognized by our ancestors. Examples from nature, art, literature, architecture, advertising, religion, and myths show the pervasiveness of these five shapes, and of the processes they represent, in the lives of people from all cultures.

Individuals can use the test on their own to discover and focus on their personal processes and interactions with others such as teachers, parents, spouses, employers, managers, colleagues and clients to better understand how humans beings live through an experience the universal processes of change embodied in these five symbols.

Sharing each other's results from the Preferential Shapes Test is an effective way for people to work together. By doing so, others can discover and explore ways in which to be supportive of the person experiencing the individuation process.

The Preferential Shapes Test provides a window on individual experiences and needs, as well as clues to the direction of the future growth. It is not intended as an index of character flaws. The process revealed by the shape preferences are part of everyone's experience. The potentials symbolized by each shape are present in everyone, although their expression in any individual is always unique.

THE PREFERENTIAL SHAPES TEST

In order to find out your present and future processes of change and growth, we invite you to take the Preferential Shapes Test. This test provides a window on individual experiences and needs, as well as clues to the direction of future growth. The potentials symbolized by each shape are present in everyone, although their expression in any individual is always unique.

"Another cross-cultural coup, Angeles has woven together the essential visual building blocks of all art, seen their primal symbolic content, and revealed the universal patterns of perception. This... skillful self-inventory layout (the Preferential Shapes Test) [is a tool] that any reader can use as a map and mirror to help identify current tendencies, conflicts, and resources that can assist one's personal growth and integration."
— Banyen Books and Sound
    Vancouver, BC, Canada

"Which shape are you? People in Angeles Arrien's workshops over the last several years have been able to answer that intriguing question by taking the "Preferential Shapes Test...." Proven to be a tool for self-discovery, the Preferential Shapes Test pinpoints a person's present internal process of growth and yields amazingly accurate results that are useful in both personal and professional pursuits."
— Body Mind Spirit Magazine

Order The Preferential Shapes Test from:
Angeles Arrien
PO Box 2077
Sausalito, CA 94966
415-331-5050 Fax: 415-331-5069
www.angelesarrien.com

(For use in workshops, quantity discounts are available.)
The Preferential Shapes Test © by Angeles Arrien 1992
Excerpted from the book,
Signs of Life: The Five Universal Shapes and How to Use Them by Angeles Arrien

For calendar of events please check our Website: www.angelesarrien.com

Concept and Design strategy:
Richard Cognata, Lucid Strategies
Design and production Flora Chang
Digital production Stacie Yawata
Paper: Fox River Paper Company
Starwhite Vicksburg, Tiara Smooth 80# cover

ISBN 0-9715002-5-8

51095

9 780971 500259